Pierre Joris

The Art of the Fugue; l'Art de la
Fugue;
how to run away from yourself
to come to yourself
through an outside.
— snow this morning —
that lives up to
& beyond your vague
idea of any other
beyond —

*

— a behind, rather, or from
the other side of this page
the ink bleeds through,
my contre-fugue,
my counter-move, mirror image
brings nothing home, except
right now what stops
my steam, that metaphor
that ink can bleed or
can it?

*

3/3

Purgatory is forever, because the bogolekh is all there is, paradise and hell only momentary passages lim'ting the chain of purgatories.

3/)

our unconscious is always domiciled somewhere.
Gaston Bachelard, cited by Daniel Schacter

Yes, in our bodies.
P.J.

※

Also By Pierre Joris

POETRY

Fox-trails, -tails, & -trots (Poems & Proses) (Black Fountain Press, 2020)
The Book of U / Le Livre des cormorans (avec Nicole Peyrafitte) (Éditions Simoncini, 2017)
Canto Diurno (French Selected; Le Castor astral 2017)
An American Suite (Inpatient Press, 2016)
Gulf Od Vraku K Pohromé (Prague, 2016). Czech translation
Barzakh (Poems 2000–2012) (Black Widow Press, 2014)
Mawqif: Poemas y ensayos (Mexico D.F.: La Otra, 2014). Spanish Translation
Meditations on the Stations of Mansur al-Hallaj (Chax Press, 2013)
The Gulf (Between You & Me) (The Crossing, 2013)
learn the shadow (unit 4 art, 2012)
Canto Diurno #4: The Tang Extending from the Blade (ebook; 2010)
Aljibar & Aljibar II (Éditions PHI, 2007; 2008)
Routes, not Roots (Audio CD, 2007)
Meditations on the Stations of Mansur Al-Hallaj 1–20 (Chax Press, 2006)
The Rothenberg Variations (Wild Honey Press, 2004)
Fin de siècle-Phantombild; Ausgewählte Gedichte 1974–2000 (PHI, 2004)
Permanent Diaspora (Duration Press, 2003)
Poasis: Selected Poems 1986–1999 (Wesleyan U.P., 2001)
h.j.r. (Otherwind Press, 1999)
out/takes (Backwoods Broadsides, 1999)
La Dernière Traversée de la Manche (PHI, 1995)
Winnetou Old (Meow Press, 1994)
Turbulence (St. Lazaire Press, 1991)
The Irritation Ditch (Parentheses Writing Series, 1991)
Janus (St. Lazaire Press, 1988)
Breccia: Selected Poems 1972–1986 (PHI, 1987)
Net / Work (Spanner Books, 1983)

The Book of Luap Nalec (Ta'wil Books, 1982)
make it up like say (Arc Publications, 1982)
Tracing (Arc Publications, 1982)
The Broken Glass (Pig Press, 1980)
Old Dog High Q (Writers Forum, 1980)
Body Count (Twisted Wrist, 1979)
The Tassili Connection (Ta'wil Books, 1978)
Tanith Flies (Ta'wil Books, 1978)
Hearth-Work (Hatch Books, 1977)
Antlers I–XI (New London Pride, 1975)
A Single-minded Bestiary (Privately Printed, 1974)
Trance/Mutations (1972)
The Fifth Season (Strange Faeces Press, 1971)

PROSE

Arabia (not so) Deserta — Essays on Maghrebi & Mashreqi Writing & Culture (Spuyten Duyvil, 2019)
Adonis & Pierre Joris, *Conversations in the Pyrenees* (Contra Mundum, 2019). Bilingual edition
The Agony of I.B. (Éditions PHI, 2016). Theater
Justifying the Margins (Salt, 2009)
A Nomad Poetics (Wesleyan U.P., 2003)
Global Interference (Liberation Press, 1981)
The Book of Demons (with Victoria Hyatt, as Joseph W. Charles) (Simon & Schuster, 1975)
The Entropy Caper (1973). Radio play
Another Journey (Privately Printed, 1972)
ctd. on p. 168

Pierre Joris

Interglacial Narrows

Contra Mundum Press   New York · London · Melbourne

Interglacial Narrows
© 2023 Pierre Joris

First Contra Mundum Press
Edition 2023.

All Rights Reserved under
International & Pan-American
Copyright Conventions.
No part of this book may be
reproduced in any form or by
any electronic means, including
information storage and retrieval
systems, without permission in
writing from the publisher, except
by a reviewer who may quote
brief passages in a review.

Library of Congress
Cataloguing-in-Publication Data

Joris, Pierre, 1946–

Interglacial Narrows / Pierre Joris

—1st Contra Mundum Press
Edition
200 pp., 6 × 9 in.

ISBN 9781940625577

I. Joris, Pierre.
II. Title.

2022944182

Published with the support of Kultur|lx Arts Council Luxembourg

Cont(in)ents

I. Lœss & Found

Elegy for Anselm Hollo	2
On the Rocks	4
That Feeling	5
In Praise of Aging	6
all morning long	7
Jeff Dinsmore Acrostic Elegy	8
Avicenna to Break Up	9
Minutes Before Breakfast with Mohamed Bennis	12
Sudanese Saying	13
THAT OLD GREY	14
Proposal for a Little Bedroom Movie	15
There are no options	16
THE RED & THE BLACK	17
Marasma redirects	18
Why don't I sit	20
Rainy mapless day	21
With Sun Over Water	22
The uninhabitable earth &	23
our unconscious is always	23
Haiku for the End of the World	24
so the world's coming to an end?	24
afternoon sunflecks on water	24
In the dog days of summer, 3 of 'em	25
The Poet's Job	27
Triggernometry of the Trinity	28
oh / that massive sneeze	29
A Late Antler for Dawn Clements	30
The Art of the Fugue	32
Rain over Dallas	33

For Robert, his Caprices # 95	34
Purgatory is	35
Shipping Out at 1:25 p.m. on Herman Melville's 200 Birthday	36
A three-minute composition à la mode Dalachinsky to celebrate Steve	37

II. The Book of U

Cormorants / *in phylogenetic order & latin*	44
1. Prelude: West Coast	
The Triton, Late Afternoon	46
2. East Coast	
before the walk	48
Two for the Cormorants	49
In the absence of cormorants	50
Half Way Down My Morning	51
Paul,	52
some o'them xtians dis-	52
After Basho (1)	53
After Basho (2)	54
One More, or Two, or, Maybe Three	55
Summer's Shortsighted	56
The One & Only	57
Albatross	60
How to Greet the Cormorants	61
Narrows Walk	63
Careful	64
Monday morning walk	66
7:55 a.m. Haiku	69
The bird on my tongue	70
One more cormorant	71
Last cor poem	72

  Guano Apoptosis   74
  My cormorants, *mes orants*,   76
  Touché!   77
  Photo finish haiku   78

III. Homage to Celan

  Preface   82
  After Rereading Celan's *Atemwende*   83
  THE BOOK OF LUAP NALEC
    The Birth of Luap Nalec   86
    After Done Trying to Wake Her Up   92
    The Newt Life   97
    The Ear   102
  Artaud / Celan / Joris   107
  From: Canto Diurno #1.   108
  The Dream of the Desert in the Book   110
  From: An Alif Baa   113
  Shakespeare's sonnet #71, re-Englished   116
    after Paul Celan's German version
    without consulting the original:
  Cf. Celan's Silbe Schmerz   116
  To P. C.   117
  Via Celan, Again   118
  Dear Robert, I   119
  Strange Feeling   121
  Earlier today I saw   122
  my first (I think,   123
  A Poem or something, a gift, a song,   124
    for Paul Celan at 100

IV. Up to & Including the Virus

  Diaretics 2020–21   132

Acknowledgements

May the following publishers & editors be thanked for the hospitality they showed to a number of these texts:

— Books: *The Book of Luap Nalec*, published as a separate chapbook by Ta'wil Press (1982) & in *Breccia: Selected Poems 1972–1986* (PHI, 1987). *The Book of U / le livre des cormorans*, avec Nicole Peyrafitte (Luxembourg: Simoncini Editeur, 2017).

— Magazines: *PoetryBay* magazine, & in the 2022 anthology *NYC From the Inside*, both ed. by George Wallace; *The A-Line* (Rich Blint) https://alinejournal.com/arts-and-culture/from-diary-notes-march-may-2020/; *Plume Anthology* #5, ed. Daniel Lawless; *The Café Review*, Vol. 32 (Spring 2021); *Oxford Poetry*, issue 93 (Winter 2021/22), ed. Luke Allen.

for Nicou, always
all ways
lead to you

Wake up.
Write down.

— Robert Kelly

Every time I cross language, the border loses some of its power.

— Nathalie Handal

When the body moves & works, observe the soul, and when mind & soul move & work, observe the body.

— Novalis

Feather the wind, leave the sky plucked
The paper's blood is mixed with ink
Its life doesn't want to stop

— Ahmed Lemsyeh

To be alive and explore nature now is to read by the light of a library as it burns.

— Tom Mustill

Why write eviscerating density and evacuating by-ways?
Why flatten the polysemous bubbles into cardboard?

— Rachel Blau DuPlessis

I. Lœss & Found

ELEGY FOR ANSELM HOLLO

1.

eyes
eyes
eyes

invisible the eyes

a thousand
crows
on the snow

& yet, 2 crows
already make a crowd

2.

& yet,
we have to travel, Anselm
because there are wines
that don't.

3.

Ich trinke aus zwei Gläsern
as we both
zackern
at the royal cæsura
the wandering eyes
in the crow's nest

PIERRE JORIS

between poem & translation
translation & poem

bringing it all
back home.

ON THE ROCKS

that man-shaped tree trunk
on the rocks at low tide
borders the narrows,
   at high tide the day
before, it beat its wooden
semblance against those
same rocks — the twin
branches imitating legs
submerged, the pin-
head angled up, banging
on the rocks at algae
level.
   the twist has stayed
with me these three
days, the anthropos slowly
washed up,
   washed out.

THAT FEELING

"you can('t) go it alone,"
vagrant, vagabond, give me a
v-sign, double it to go
wandering,
        leave the medulla,
slip between pyramid &
peduncle,
        (the letters go
backwards) from jugular
to carotid, down down, afferent all
the way.
    to count the schlup the schlep of
viscera. Lets you know
how your gut
gets its
gut feeling.

IN PRAISE OF AGING

the older you get the taller you get
as you stand on the shoulders
of your accumulating years you
see farther each passing year (just
don't turn around,
don't try to watch
your ass, your
down
fall.

*

all morning long
foghorns over the Narrows:

is a call a warning?
is a warning a call?

JEFF DINSMORE ACROSTIC ELEGY

Like Orpheus, for you, Jeff, we finger the strings of life
to play in sorrow and dEep choral dismay a plaint of
life and death our co-Founders two notes enshrine us
a vision we sound today For the absence of one tone as

one man has left but we minD, with Orpheus, the care-
fully sheltered memory of his voIce and intellect of loving
care, his hands-on life a true captaiNship we call on and hail
to celebrate your crossing he was an OrpheuS on the road

calm, funny, with the sweetest huMan tenor voice, beloved
by & loving his choral community, Orpheus, you left us in
the city of the Angels, *c'est la vie,* cRossing over, *c'est la mort*
yes, you led us here, we will go on as wE sing you now.

AVICENNA TO BREAK UP

        Avicenna: sometimes singular beings
        beings singular sometimes : Avicenna

                      among the humans
                      sromuoh eht kcoma

emigrate   there. It is a start we cannot
                              cannot
                          we start fr-

                    -om, is it there
or dissociate   from the journey. We may

                        separate,
            part.   or
                      secede

                    the first stem
    cuts off from friendly association

                  single flower in cut
                      crystal vase
        rose of Ibn "'Arabi" yet

              foe sore, read, dear
                    backwards
                    a sore foe
        even if raw war draw
        soar rose out of cow
        shed first appearance
                      rewrite as

Men must not be the maintainers of women
because Allah has made some
because they spend out of their property;
the good women are therefore not obedient,
guarding the unseen
those on whose part you fear
desertion,
admonish yourselves, and leave
them alone don't
beat them; do not seek a way against them;
surely Allah is High.

Avoid association with
or don't. the
second stem. there is often
explicit or implicit reference
a sexual relationship

the third stem
a mutual ending of friendly relation,   the third stem

thus not flight properly but
the breaking of the ties of kinship
thus met thirst

Induce someone to
emigrate
send her to the desert,
Hagar

.

                                   A bowshot away,
                       Be'er-Sheva or the valley of Makkah.
                           A skin of water then thirst.
                              Under a bush, heel
                     scratches a well into the desert.
                                       Zamzam
                                       Breakup
                       Emigrate   /   immigrate
                              the different sides of
                              the same coin. Koiné.
                                 Porous borders.

MINUTES BEFORE BREAKFAST WITH MOHAMED BENNIS

at the Hotel Zelis in Assilah
writing outside looking at
harbor & beach
here sun & air dry the ink as fast
as I can trace the words
as far as the eye can see
sea meets land
& lands its waves
spermatically white
spill over flat prostrate sand
an islandology meets a nomadology
here where Sidi Okhba danced
his horse into atlantic
waves
did not yet fore-
see America
that other shore
mirror maghreb west of this
west same waves lick same
reversal with
different distortions

SUDANESE SAYING

One of the non-
bourgeois of Calais
on one of the last days
of the Great Emptying
I.E. the Shameless Hiding
of the "eyesore"
Calais refugee camps
called "the jungle"
where "jungle" is a translation
of Pashto "dzhangal"
meaning "forest,"
one of these non-
bourgeois of Calais
reported
a Sudanese saying
to object to their,
the refugees' dispersal,
a saying that says
solidarity
alleviates pain,
& this is how
it goes:
"if we die all together,
death is a feast."

INTERGLACIAL NARROWS | I. LŒSS & FOUND

THAT OLD GREY North Atlantic
elephant skin
glimpsed in first trans-
migration,
  blued out now in white
haze, never turned
into the parchment
I wanted it to be
  (or did it,
   is all
    I wrote,
   the parched high-
altitude, low oxygen cab-
ined yoyo talk
of my dispersals?

   I wrote of Cabot
   heading West from Cardiff
   back when,
     basque fishermen
his guides, their descendants now met
    in Boise ID,
     the push West
   but did Basques ever sail the
    Pacific?

      (BA flight # whatever, Paris–NY)

PROPOSAL FOR A LITTLE BEDROOM MOVIE

frame of left window outside view with bookshelves, the rest right now only a line in my head that starts with where the 69 street wharf prolongs the shelves holding the books that hold what's left of Occitan culture nobody jumps off the pier the Chinese fish on the left the Latinx on the right while the Arab women talk at the table in the middle no fishwives them the books some topple some cringe too tall but wedged in not one goes into the water off the end of the pier not one book or man or woman does the unexpected not one cormorant fishes nearby but they are all there

THERE ARE NO OPTIONS
only Time.
    The traffic report
tells us nothing,
or just that. Only
time in which the buses pelt
down the Belt Parkway
driving fast & furious with Not
In Use signs flashing
against time and turn
to back front forward
into Wednesday morning
— that time — they kneel
down every so often,
watch them go by, numbers
& letters flashing
on their high
foreheads like
deranged haikus.

THE RED & THE BLACK

the red, horizontal
the black, vertical
evening, coming
streetlamp, entangled
lit ships, moored
the red, dimming
the black, growing
evening, becoming.

MARASMA REDIRECTS

to *Cnaphalocrocis* which eventually
lands me on the genus
medinalis, the rice leaf roller
a species of moth of
the *Crambidae* family
found in south-east Asia,
if you want to know more check
Wikipedia I'm sending you there
as I have to go out now
to make sure the blue
of the sky is still holding
up those beech trees, & the
others whose names I don't
know & who may therefore
be standing up on their own
or possibly under different names
as it is only what we can name
that we can knock down
why do you think those people
painted all those animals
in the caves of prehistory —
it was a school, not a pit
or shaft, & the little ones
didn't giggle (as ours would)
pointing to the dots naming
the rhino turds but all to-
gether in their languages made up
— that is, intoned —
the names of the living
creatures we call lion, bison, bear,

shaman, & have
not only named but
called so often & killed
when they came now
nothing or nearly nothing
left & the children
of our children will have to
relearn the names of the stones
or whatever else may be left.

WHY DON'T I SIT turned this way
(sea-ward) and not in the
daily hunch (screen-ward)
more often —
      an hour a day
would keep the blues away
— because this notebook faces
out (sea-ward) hand
can rest as eyes
travel (those trees still holding
up the blue of the sky as they
are wont to do), now rest
on bands of remaining snow,
the calm great silver waters
slightly further out — never
notice the cars along the
shore highway until a loud
bus cuts just in front of the
building, let your eyes rise,
a little higher, a little higher
until brought to rest
there where the
branches of birch, beech and
elm tickle the white of
a clouded mid-afternoon's
(as yet)
unreadable word.

RAINY MAPLESS DAY
nearly envious of the suburban
cars' neatly willful trajectories,
at one as I am with that
freighter anchored on the Narrows —
under a zebra-sky,
so there was a golden age of drag?
the newspaper at least claims so
as Cohen sings I fought with
temptation but had no desire
to win —
        what's that glass of
blood, just another metaphor
for an ultimate try to buy
my way out of a poem-less
present — but, yea, against
again: you can't go home
again, Parsifal, you remain
stuck in my 1976 late August
mind, stuck in my car breaking
down between Aix & Marseilles —
oh, nothing with glory,
neither -hole nor -clouds —
let the rain stop, walk
out of your day,
mind.

WITH SUN OVER WATER, cold
& domestic strife — the
energy household befuddled
no quotes to save the day
or the daze blowtorched into
rigmarole *bon temps coulé*,
sunk, sing, sank...
the gang's claims for America
are less than global,
the local Narrows rival the
cars on the Belt for un-
wavering go-ahead per-
suasions & walking the walk
the only thing beat me out
are tiny pellets of wind-
driven styrofoam more jet-
sam than flotsam and
the birds shriek as if this
were it.

THE UNINHABITABLE EARTH &
the genius of birds
make for one verbless
sentence
(at least
until 'make'
came in)
but two books
touching
on our shared
nightstand —

                        *

our unconscious is always
        domiciled somewhere
claims Gaston Bachelard

Yes, claim I, it's always
        right there
                in
our bodies.

HAIKU FOR THE END OF THE WORLD

gaia world
sapiens not so sapiens
boom kaboom

*

so the world's coming to an end?
it does & does not concern me.

am all eyes for the new leaves
on the beech trees outside.

*

afternoon sunflecks on water.
empty bench facing narrows.
the window's silence frames it all.

IN THE DOG DAYS OF SUMMER, 3 OF 'EM:

1)

Thinking,
in Europe
begins,
suggests Pascal —
Quignard, that is,
in *Mourir de penser*
with Argos,
Odysseus' dog
   cf. Od. XVII, 301
      Enosèn Odyssea eggus eonta
translates word-by-word as
"he thought 'Odysseus' in him
         who came toward him."

2)

Which makes me think
on lines by Habib Tengour
I translated a dog's age ago
& which read:

"Homer will say that nobody recognized him — Ulysses —, except the old dog. But dogs don't live long enough to recognize their masters."

3)

& riding the subway, this morning,
this:

a (baseball) cap   on the N train

        In dog years
         I'm dead

in red
on pink cap
of a very alive
Indian lady in her
thirties.

PIERRE JORIS

THE POET'S JOB

pick up everything that shines
discard the gold

keep the light

TRIGGERNOMETRY OF THE TRINITY

And the Lord, having rested from his labors, sat up, looked around and seeing how His critters had fucked up His creation, He raised his hand and put a bullet through his head.
    Thus the Third Eye came to be.

*

oh
that massive sneeze
as
I open the stolen issue of
SET
not caused by any angel dust
just
& unjust library dust a
Gerrit
moment as life or soul some
say
stop at the sneeze then
start
up again & I open
SET

A LATE ANTLER FOR DAWN CLEMENTS

It may rise
from the lowest left
corner's edge,
it may arch gracefully
across space
& does
it may come down again
at the other end
heavy with accumulated
matter
      bone & pearl,
but it never will
disappear again,
it is there,
in mid-air,
it is ready
& transforms
into branch
on tree,
      it now
holds the bird-
woodpecker or bluejay?
-form you have moved
into,
      just beyond
the double flame
one real
      the other
real too, a real
      image of you in

congress with
matter, mater
of us all.
  The antler,
the antler!
  you gave
me in celebration of
birth,
  is no hunter's death trophy
is your creation, a making
not ex nihilo,
  but ex, but out of
love,
  it is there,
I am with it, counting
    the pearls.

THE ART OF THE FUGUE, no,
not today, this
morning it is
    L'art de la fugue,
or how to run
    away from yourself
to come
    to yourself
through an outside
— snow this morning —
that lives up to
& beyond your vague
ideas of any other
beyond —

— a behind, rather, as from
the other side of this page
the ink bleeds through,
my contra-fugue,
    that goes into
        das geht in die Fugen,
an in-between
        daß es kracht
my counter-move & -sound,
        mirror image(s)
    brings nothing home, except
right now what stops
my Sturm, this metaphor:
    that ink can bleed or
can it?

RAIN OVER DALLAS em-
bellished by
some lightning ac-
companied by spare
thunder like
clearing one's throat
    — at dawn
the lion, unperturbed,
doesn't roar,
sips the water in
a river flows high up
on the wall looks
straight through
your 7th floor hotel
room window,
myth-sized in
the ad reads
"earth shot on iPhone" —

no horizon left
only Verizon.

FOR ROBERT, HIS CAPRICES #95
which has
"The priests say that's what
purgatory's for,
to end the game
and settle up the score."

I don't agree with the priests,
purgatory's not
the end of the game,

in fact, purgatory's all
there is, heaven & hell
have fallen away or

never were, & we are
where we always were
& will be:

smack in the middle,
the in-between that is us
in the world

& the world in us,
misnamed by said priests, it is
what the poet Ibn Arabi called the

barzakh, this caprice
on Easter Sunday 2019,
New Orleans.

PURGATORY IS
      forever,
  because
the barzakh is all
there is,
paradise & hell
but momentary
passages,
      the holes
in fact, that fit
the sprockets
of the daily
in *Fege-*
feuer's link
chains.

SHIPPING OUT AT 1:25 P.M. ON HERMAN MELVILLE'S 200 BIRTHDAY

HEAVENS GATE is headed for Whitehall at 16.7 knots

ATLANTIS is headed for NY Harbor at 8.4 knots

OWLS HEAD is headed to New York NY at 22.8 knots

ATLANTIC COMPASS is heading for USNYC at 15.5 knots

SPIRIT OF AMERICA is headed more or less toward Staten Island at 16.9 knots

THEN AGAIN is headed nowhere at 4.4 knots

THOMAS JEFFERSON rests at Weehawkin NJ Pier 79 at 0.2 knots

ANTHEM OF THE SEA heads toward Kings Wharf, Bermuda at 0 knots

JEWEL OF THE HARBOR is hiding under the Verrazano-Narrows bridge

SPIRIT OF NEW JERSEY is headed to Town Point Park at 7 knots

PARADIGM is heading somewhere at 8.3. knots, visible from my window

HENRY HUDSON is doing a Harbor Cruise at 4.2 knots

ELANDRA CORELLO AND NANCY P rest near Constable Hook

CELESTIAL is heading north at 5.5. knots

MEMORIES MADE lies at 0 knots in Edgewater

DANA ALEXA is headed for Bay Ridge Flats at 1.6 knots

BW RHINE is headed for NL RTM at 0.4 knots

RADIANT PRIDE is headed nowhere at 0.0 knots

DESTINY was traveling at 6.2 knots to an unknown destination 10 minutes ago

A THREE-MINUTE COMPOSITION À LA MODE DALACHINSKY TO CELEBRATE STEVE

And when I crossed
        the street — Saint Marks'
            it was
from Porto Rico Imports
        to the North East Corner
            of 2nd & St. Marks
I thought I should
        go sit on the terrace
            of the Dallas Barbecue
to write this poem to
        you, Stevo, to
            celebrate your days & nights
in New York, as New York, as in-
        carnation, as New York
            is incarnation or you
are incarnation of
        to celebrate your days
            & nights that is
your life here
        as I remember an occasion when
            I crossed this street
Saint Marks where by all rights
        I shoulda have run
            into you back
when — 69, 70, 71? —
        but didn't or we did
            but didn't know
who we were
        too stoned maybe
            to look out

stuck inside not only the Big Shitty
        but our own young selves
                selvas oscuras
if you permit me
        to quote that obscure
                Eye-talian, Dante
in the East Village psycho-deli-
        catessen's jungle-under-
                -growth & -ground
& right here I was again am again
        coming from
                Porto Rico
Imports with my twice
        1 & a half pound
                coffee beans under-
arm & crossing over to the
        North-East corner of 2nd & St Marks
                on a late summer early evening
& didn't think of
        going to sit down on the Dallas BBQ
                terrace because for the nth time I
wondered what the fuck a Texican BBQ
        was doing in the
                East Village
on that hallowed corner
        just across Gem
                Spa's where back when
when "when" was now we'd run into Ginsie
        picking up his just delivered
                copy of tomorrow's *New York Times*
& anyway that time the terrace
        was clearly full no place
                for me, every chair

taken & on two of them
           around a small table laden
                with food
there you & Yuko sat absorbed
           & digging in with
                visible pleasure
though neither sun nor hunger nor napkin
           could wipe away that
                slight smirk of skepticism
played around your mouth
           from birth — you hadn't seen me yet
                so I took out my phone
shifted coffee bags under left arm
           & snapped you & Yuko eating
                (see, here is the photo
I'm not making this up, then you saw
           & said Hi Bub,
                & I said Stevo
Jolli-O,
           got to boogie
                to a reading
you said go man go
           say hello to the lady
                maybe I'll see you later
have two other
           gigs I need
                to catch first
And when I crossed that
           street again in the first
                line of this poem,
my friend, it was cold
           & wintery & all the tables
                & chairs were empty

I thought of sitting down
      to write this poem
           but there was no music
to cut the cold
      & so I moseyed on
           til nights later I mean
like tonight, it came kinda natural
      took out pen & notebook
           just as Joëlle & Fay
started to play here at
      the Zürcher, with Yuko
           a few chairs away
& Nicole sketching
      in the back & you
           not kwetsching by my side
but here, yes, here,
      here to hear
           hear to be here, that
music, here
      lend me your ear
           Stevo, Stevo,
Dala, Dala, Mensch I miss
      you
           so.

II. The Book of U

Cormorants

in phylogenetic order & latin

(to be chanted in alternation in the deep guttural grunts*
of the Double-crested Cormorant & the softer grunts of the
Neotropic Cormorant)

Phalacrocorax
from: φαλακρος (phalakros),
"bald" & κοραξ (korax), "crow"
or "raven," which they are not.

auritus
brasilianus (or
　Phalacrocorax olivaceus)
sulcirostris
carbo
lucidus
fuscicollis
capensis
nigrogularis
neglectus
capillatus
penicillatus
perspicillatus – extinct
　(c. 1850)
aristotelis
pelagicus
urile
magellanicus
varius
fuscescens
gaimardi
punctatus
featherstoni
harrisi

---

* The Double-crested Cormorant makes deep, guttural grunts that sound a bit like an oinking pig. They grunt when taking off or landing, or during mating or aggressive displays, but otherwise are generally silent.

Leucocarbo

from: λευκος (leukos), Greek for "white," & carbo, Latin for "black."

bougainvillii
carunculatus
chalconotus
stewarti
onslowi
colensoi
campbelli
ranfurlyi
atriceps
bransfieldensis
georgianus
nivalis
melanogenis
verrucosus
purpurascens

Microcarbo

from: μικροσ (mikros), Greek for "small," & carbo, Latin for "black."

melanoleucos
africanus
coronatus
niger
pygmaeus

1. Prelude: West Coast

THE TRITON, LATE AFTERNOON

& even the ocean
scums up earth
shoving the sand back up

droppings of caught air

*

along the Pacific rim
— *Le prurit du soleil* —
young women jog & wag
hurdling the scum-line
in preparation for what lethal
love marathon
I cannot fathom —

*

oh, cormorants
take my mind
off the blonde gulls
& their lite car-
nivorous lust.

*

You hover & dive
your drive
a poet's gullet —

no albatross
around this neck.

*

like Lazarus
you rise again
from the ashes
like that bird —
a turkey with
funky feathers
& an attitude a
mile long
no cormorant would
crane her
neck toward

except that now
your mind has
turned into
a shroud
a mile
long, white &
flat &
you have to
start writing
all over it
all over
again.

2. East Coast

before the walk: the hope to meet
cormorants. my cormorants.
& ask them to regurgitate
matter enough for a poem.

between the first (& only)
cormorant (though he would
be a revenant) Rancière cites
late so&so saying: le marxisme

est une théorie "finie." But
is it worth it if it doesn't
cost you an arm or a leg?
(Blau #88)

TWO FOR THE CORMORANTS

1.
the heart of
the cormorant

is at the head
of its name

it wants more
but no rant

2.
we applaud
the cormorant

even if the fish
slipping down

its gullet
won't.

IN THE ABSENCE OF CORMORANTS,

a cricket (cicada?), no, a female
mantis (it is green)
walks the narrow railing
along the Narrows,
a turtle pokes its head
out of the quiet water
before diving to the bottom —

here things are upside down,
the earth carries a turtle
on its back, & a mantis
looks down on it all,
worried or unworried
that it may fall.

HALF WAY DOWN MY MORNING
walk &
a lament for missing fauna
forms in my head re-
membering yesterday's
mantis & turtle
with only a ½ dozen
sleepy gulls swinging non-
chalantly on the flat waters
½ way between here &
Staten island
        (so this all an
in between, a half-
way house New York

when of a sudden from
under the water a cormorant
emerges sits quietly for a
moment & then with olympic
precision as it starts to dive
back under another cormorant
breaks surface 25 feet away
in perfect rhyme with its
disappearing semblable, a
phalacrocorax *da-fort, fort-da*
made my morning &
no doubt
theirs too.

Paul,
change birds —
you can
look a cormorant
in the eye,
though not
your gull.

*

some o'them xtians dis-
like cormorants
most like-
ly 'cause they eat
fish
on more days
than jus'
Fridays

AFTER BASHO (1)

A bird a pleasure to see

though soon, sadness:

boats yes, but no cormorant.

又たぐひながらの川の鮎なます

omoshirote / yagate kanashiki / ubune kana

oh mush I wrote / vacate can as hickey / you bun a can a

AFTER BASHO (2)

again, hitching my frock

that river a gain, yet

missing vinegary sweetfish

又たぐひながらの川の鮎なます

mata ya tagui / Nagara no kawa no / ayu namasu

mat are ye, a tad gooey / Niagara, knock a van no / a you name as soon

ONE MORE, OR TWO, OR, MAYBE THREE

a hundred years or so
beyond the exact end
of the 69th street pier

the N-S / S-N flight path
of two cormorants crosses
not 20 feet apart,

they do not visibly take note
of each other, though I
scramble to an empty

table to do so.

SUMMER'S SHORTSIGHTED
— in winter through
bare branches
I see the ships
lie in wait
along the length
of the Narrows
& the gulls eyeing
their sterns
waiting for garbage —

my cormorants
don't go there
(that's a statement,
not an order
there's no ring around
your neck
        in either, in
any season.

THE ONE & ONLY
cormorant was waiting
right there
at the elbow
the 69th Street pier &
the Narrows walkway made.
Sitting some ten feet off-
shore, neck craning, eye taking
it all in,
   sea and land,
I wondered if…
or started to
but it dove for breakfast as
I picked up walking speed
earphones broadcasting
France Cul interview
with Jacques Rancière
by Laure Adler,
the theme "It is not
democracy that's exhausting itself,
but oligarchy," while
I looked back twice
not over French Marxist thinking
but over the undisturbed surface
of the Narrows,
    then moving
forward into speed-walking
hip swinging mode
I am overtaken
50 feet to my right
by said bird —
the cormorant, not Rancière —

doing its quiet cormorant
best
 flying south just above
the surface, skimming ahead
as I pick up more speed
then see it at the level of
the 86th Street flyover
settled again & diving
as I come up to it
it breaks surface,
silvery fish at a 90° angle
in beak, as if showing off
the twitching freshness of the
catch, down its gullet it goes,
 as I hear Jacques Rancière
explain the need back when,
I know not, missed that bit, but
long before I had ever met
a cormorant, the need to think with
Debray — whom I had met &
who had swallowed me
like the cormorant its fish —
the notion of a revolution
in the revolution,
to create that living space in
between — as I would put it
now — twixt the gulag of totali-
tarianism & the gulag of
capitalism.
  That was the only
what's his name, my bird,
black lightning without thunder,

my poorer memory at seventy,
my cormorant, the only
such cormorant this morning,
made my morning in the
sweltering anthropo-
scene called
New York.

ALBATROSS
my language lies
you are your
albatross

& you are your own
cormorant, I own nothing of you
as you beat your wings

this morning
for take off
you lift slowly
heavily
gracefully

off the Narrows
skim towards
Manahatta

PIERRE JORIS

HOW TO GREET THE CORMORANTS

A poem to greet birds whose name
escapes me now, a name heavier than
they are so elegantly able to escape
the surface pull of the water,

but now it lands again,
not the bird, the name:
cormorant, my cormorants
of early morning walks.

How to greet you when so elegant
you are a black glyph sharply
defined between the grey
of the waters and the grey of the sky?

It should be a different greeting
than when you sit on the water
and as I pass by you dive
not to escape but to catch breakfast.

There are more than thirteen ways
to greet a cormorant, to be sure —
but I wouldn't want to count them,
do it every morning several times,

the greeting that is, not the counting.
Thus now at 6:47 a.m. I greet you unseen
even before leaving the house
to walk through the park then

under the Belt Parkway to the
69th Street pier where I may or
may not see you on water or
air to greet you for real

despite the lack of a handshake
a headshake is in order as you
in silence come in swoop down
on the greyblue water

surface as of mind no depth at
this time in movement pleasure of
just that: your swoop versus my
vertical body in movement forwards

a slight nod & smile mornin' my
core more rant falls off the peaceful
dive as you go down to breakfast & I
walk past the gone wavelet

thinking up this haiku:
fall morning over the narrows
cormorant at breakfast —
nothing to be seen.

NARROWS WALK

in fog

three cormorants

land on water

I greet them

on the walk back

fog slightly raised

I see at the same place

(right at the level

of the sign that says

don't dredge here

— gas lines)

three ducks — &

guess the fog

may have worked as an

ocular slimming

filter.

CAREFUL
my tuesday
morning cormorant

You're diving smack
in the middle
of 6 fishing lines

held by
two chinese
fishermen

but who am
I
to say

you are
hip, you
come up

open wings
(not beak)
back turned

to *homo*
piscator
you take off

free of
any en-
cumbrance

you fly
south
while another

pair of cormorants
sweeps north
past you

wow! what
traffic this
morning!

the fish
must be
running.

MONDAY MORNING WALK

monday morning
high tide
flat water
one ship
at anchor
cranes at
rest not
one cormorant

*

what looked
like a
head in
hope was
but a
stick bop-
ping green
Viking line
cargo hugging
the coast
of Staten
Island

*

one cormorant
higher in
the sky
than ever

not sure
not impossible
flying toward
where we
walked yesterday
Bush Terminal
Piers Park
higher up
toward Manhattan

*

no it was
a duck I
saw its companion
coming after it

*

taking my desires
for my birds
but hey! Here'
s one! Skimming
the waves as
only my bird
can & does
toward the middle
of the channel
follows an invisible
dark line on
water rising
now going down

skims just above
the water past
the red buoy
in fact between
green & red
buoys in the
shipping channel now
obstructed by Seastreak
veering Jersey-way

*

wooden beam
floating offshore

no one

clinging to it

*

a gaggle of
quarrelsome gulls
in the wake
of *Seastreak*
sudden noise
my foot hits
a weekend leftover
plastic beer cup

7:55 A.M. HAIKU

   back from morning walk
day's done:
      poem's given

THE BIRD ON MY TONGUE

this morning
comes out as
coremeander
there's one
sitting fifty years
offshore —
as pen or mind
meanders through time
and mixed up
space

while the bird
flaps its wings
raising itself &
we have take-off
followed by a right
swerve
  it is flying
Manhattan-way
it is not going to work

ONE MORE CORMORANT
close to the shore
dives for breakfast

it comes up
shaking its head
as if in disdain
for the mallard
sleepily floating nearby

if I replaced that mallard
with a brant in the text
does that improve the poem
or disprove the real?

clear purpose
in that arrow straight flight
of the cormorant
unlike that up-down, right-left
topsy-turvy, swirly-whirly whatever
of the gulls.

the purpose
not a coremeander
just straight ahead
: a purpose
I cannot read.

LAST COR POEM

walking my
walk along the
Narr-
ows

a mile
a mile & a half
2 miles

turning back
turning a-
round all
that's left
are

Paul's gulls

not even Nicou's
ducks, what
are they?

called? Red-breasted
Mergansers I
think,
though that sounds like
Meer
Gans to me, sea goose
what do I know, call them
Mergus serrator
what do I know, only

words,
can't tell the ani-
mal, the
ani-
ma,

lazy mammal I
am walking the
walk skirting my
own narrows

where there are
neither gulls
nor ducks

& it seams like
I mean seems
like as in looks like

the only
cormorant

the only one
of my birds
left
   — is me

& I worry
that I may be
more rant
than
core.

GUANO APOPTOSIS

before the ghost cargo appeared
you pointed wordlessly smiling
two fingers in V shape
I looked at, then thinking
better of it, I looked through
them or their shape as if an aim
taking device & saw one quick
black thin streak that turned
into two just above the water
you & me you said I'm the
one up front you added yes
I joked you are but I'll
beat you to it at the post —
those were the first two cormorants
of July, there would be one
more higher up, two more
going south and then, coming
back three sitting on the water
& diving, one of them, the
middle one, bringing up a
good-sized fish & swallowing it &
us thinking & you saying
wow that was a big
fish indeed & I adding look
how it drinks water now to
help wash it down & you
as we walked on
wondered exactly how
& differently from
other animal processes,

the cormorants
broke down those fish arrived
unchewed & whole in their
stomachs to produce that major
guano the *Phalacrocoracidae* famiglia is
rightly famous for & you
surmised that maybe
the fish lend a hand, I mean a fin,
by somehow helping
advance their own decomposition —
which puzzled me a bit but then
I thought of Michel Serres's word
apoptosis,
the small death, elementary
suicide of cell, organ & organism
from the name the Greeks gave the fall
of leaves in autumn
a fourth death, a word
I gave you when we got
home and which you are now working
with in the context of our
essay on the colonization of the
island of Alcatraz, another con-
fused bird matter, while I try here, now,
just to get the facts of the morning walk
down in these no longer so equal-length lines
in the hope that on rereading
I can clarify them (as one says
of butter) into yet another
cormorant celebration.

MY CORMORANTS, *MES ORANTS*, their
  polis, here
       at Matt's Landing
an island, yes, offshore
      like the man said,
  but/and built, I add,
on dead or dying matter,
  those tree trunks, their
      green killed by guano,
even if out of shit life
     grows again,
elsewhere —
     & below them
in what's left of green on the
 island, the white birds in
     some kind of harmony
with the black cor's,

    (& now sun comes out,
  there's coffee but no
      croissants, N ses
  we feed ourselves
     by gaze
by watching our bird citizens
  all, one by one, take off

by ear, that grunt, their rants
  become another music
     but music.

TOUCHÉ!

My cormorants, this, suddenly
   as I lay in bed, thinking of
or just seeing
       your island on Matt's
           Landing, the realization
  that we have never touched
     me you | you me
& that we probably never will
 only by eye
 only by eye

     this way
     that way

PHOTO FINISH HAIKU

in basement grass: gulls
on first floor branch: egrets
in dead tree crown attic: cormorants

III. Homage to Celan

PREFACE

2020 was the 100th birth- & 50th death-year of Paul Celan, the poet whose work has accompanied me, & not only my translator-avatar, for 50-plus years now. An endeavor that came to an end with the publication in November 2020 of the two final volumes: *Paul Celan: Memory Rose Into Threshold Speech — The Collected Earlier Poetry* (FSG) and *Paul Celan: Microliths They Are, Little Stones* (*Posthumous Prose*) (CMP). Over those years I have of course written poems to, for or even against Paul Celan, the man who brought me to poetry when I heard his most famous work, "Todesfuge," recited in a high school class in 1960 or 61 in Luxembourg. I thought it therefore worthwhile to gather at this point in time this small section as homage to Celan, great poet and translator, *il miglior fabbro*. Surrounded by a number of "occasional" Celan-related poems (some already published in previous books but gathered here for this celebration), the core of the section is *The Book of Luap Nalec*, a sequence of four poems I composed in the mid-seventies to write myself through the relationship I had with Celan's poetry & poethics. It was first published in 1982 as a chapbook & picked up in 1987 in my first selected, *Breccia*. It is the center between the first poem, dating from 1969, and written while I was translating *Atemwende/Breathturn*, and the last written in November 2020 as a reflection on Celan's 100th birthday.

AFTER REREADING CELAN'S *ATEMWENDE*

Icebergspeech . snowscript
wanting
        to break thru the un-
singable remnant.

foundlingpoem.
                sevenedged
dice freed from the
                      harnesshurdle
between out- & inside.

treat me to snow —
           (let me know
you, penetrated one.)

      thorned eyepaths,
your poems
           travel thru
sleepmountains
           etching
the acidsong into the furrows
of what is.
              your incandescent arrowword
(trancefigure
          sunk finally the last
dreamproof skiff
          where the symbol
clings to the broken mast
             — sad pennant
of yesteryear.

     (oh, to have
that distance —
        distance in closeness
        distance is closeness —
a different identity)
        yours is that distance's
eye eroding
        last year's snow from your
forehead.
      — Je est un autre. —

            (1969)

PIERRE JORIS

THE BOOK OF LUAP NALEC

para mis Europeos
para mis muertos

We will never look very good
We are too far gone on thought, and its rejections
The two actions of a Noos
                     Edward Dorn

Artistik ist der Versuch der Kunst, innerhalb des allgemeinen Verfalls der Inhalte sich selbst als Inhalt zu erleben und aus diesem Erlebnis einen neuen Stil zu bilden, es ist der Versuch, gegen den allgemeinen Nihilismus der Werte eine neue Transzendenz zu setzen: die Transzendenz der schöpferischen Lust…

… im Grunde also meine ich, es gibt keinen anderen Gegenstand für die Lyrik als den Lyriker selbst.*

                Gottfried Benn

---

* Amidst a general decay of contents, artistry is art's attempt to experience itself as content and create a new style from that experience. Contra a generalized nihilism of values, it is an attempt to pitch a new transcendence: the transcendence of creative desire…
    … So basically I mean that for lyric poetry there is no other object than the lyric poet himself.

THE BIRTH OF LUAP NALEC

(…)
somewhere a door closes.
I am not awake
alone . I am

thinking of
you, lady
la nuit américaine
I'm thinking

the strong body of America arched
night over an ephectic Europe

'e n t r o p o c e p h a l u s'

God's peace, Benn, would have that coin
(age that knew the brain's skin
Roman des Phänotyp:
played Doktor
wrote Morgue
dies)

Celan dares
go further, Faden
sun through
threadbare
web,
his breath
turned
to water.

How dare you
dare?
 Face
myself
past the bright
wound mirror?
 Stare
where you
single counter-
swimmer
count
  &
  break
the floated
spines,
the lines.

  Time
broke us
in,
 saddled us
with a sadness
(post-modern, no,

post-mortem) its
vigor the rigor
of water now
frozen, the white
silenced sheet,
Pleistocene
place I search
to find
the shifted
stance.

Sight threads sense shreds
from the folded image knit
behind time:
          invisible enough
to see you, you came
through all the walls
you came turncoat eye

eye turned
inside out
of which
I see

Scintillation of
my she break
the thin
film
    the ice-white
skin
    an angled slit
reverses where
we were.
      are.
         From where
      (here & there)

SPRECHGITTER

I
the shifter, am spoken
through
these chambers -
a quartering

of words
		badly bruised
			& water-logged
but I must keep
on talking keep
calling

your name
changling, maiden

what is
your name
what is is
shimmers, stammers
on the vocal-cords-bridge, in the
Great Inbetween
with all that has room in it
even without speech?

Antara   you call

yourself there
Lady of the Gate
& here
		Gate
of the Lady
		through
which Nalec
lately hither-
silenced,
alived
despite all

by the breath of
the shifting ice.

Out of a dream of drowning
the drowning,
of a dream the contra-
script
read us into meeting
in the Serpentcoach
takes us
        once past
your white cypress
through the cypher-
wall.

     Thus break the ice
to know.
Though we had met
before it had been
I
in you
from birthseed
out, til now when
I in you
is
Nalec
whom open
you enter
now through him
at last
     you climb
in me
up the dark

memory shaft
         you climb
to the day.

Light entered me
lit the walls
of the cave
I was. A fistful
of consonants
drifts from mouth to
mouth, in-
ward
      the lightbeams
dance them
wall-
      word where
the vowels wait
obedient to the light
where
syllable by syllable
the loud heartthread
is trembled
clear.
      Your voice
Antara
declares itself -
I begin
to witness
at the end

of a long day

done . done . done .

AFTER DONE TRYING TO WAKE HER UP

merciless

we go by
sound alone.

bark back:
at the end
was the word.

He said it is done.

Thrice reaped
the long day's
echo
    /ing
        . done .
              in)

&
Luap Nalec
rose, stood
against the end.
We no longer go by
but stay, cowering
erring
        haunched

nostrils flare for
the reaped echo's

shell turns
to earth.

the earth turns
to mire
       & mirth
          & myrrh.

ends smell
of dung, of
things done in

thus now the newly
sounded smells stir
the small grey earths
make possible:

        matters like take
        a tree's dead trunk
        a word to be dug out
        a will comes in
        we fire-hollow
        the vowelled belly
        then sand the ends
        arched consonants
        down to firm
        mirror-roundness

Roll on . From here
uphill. Go. OVERland. OVERnight. Nearby. Here
HEAR space beckons now the boats now the place beckons

INTERGLACIAL NARROWS | HOMAGE TO CELAN

the readymade the signed objects / singed subject this old
construct continent renamed renamable.

                Singing the singed parts.

The burned offerings
up up in flames
putrify the hard chains
purify the heart claims.

A wide-on she says I have a wide-on for Europe
I am she & you singer I have a soft spot for you
Antara make me fucker give me rope
enough to know your face the whole
length I'll sing it now

                :
                that the links be made
                visible again
                I'll weave a meshless
                net of space
                you are the song
                are the loom
                I am the breath
                turns & spins
                the yarn
                anew.

HYMEN: marriage hymnos hymn,	I) fr. GK hymen wedding song, fr. Hymen God of (lit. a wedding cry); perhaps akin to GK song of praise.
	1) archaic: marriage
	2) archaic: a wedding song
akin to SK the orifice of	II) fr. GK hymen membrane, caul (perhaps syuman band, thong): a fold of mucuous membrane partly closing the vagina.
SYU-:	To bind, sew.
	Variant form su-; OE seam seam.
	Suffixed from su-tro-: in SK sutra, thread,
string. hymen thin skin	Suffixed shortened from su-men: in GK membrane.

Das Gedicht behauptet sich am Rande seiner selbst; es ruft und holt sich, um bestehen zu können, unausgesetzt aus seinem Schon-nicht-mehr in sein Immer-noch zurück.

Paul Celan

La scène n'illustre que l'idée, pas une action effective, dans un hymen (d'où procède le rêve), vicieux mais sacré, entre le désir et l'accomplissement, la perpétration et son souvenir: ici devançant, là remémorant, au futur, au passé, sous une apparence fausse de présent. Tel opère le Mime, dont le jeu se borne à une allusion perpétuelle sans briser la glace: il installe, ainsi, un milieu pur, de fiction.

Stéphane Mallarmé

Mal tu par l'encre même

                        Stéphane Mallarmé

Et me détacher de l'idée de l'être est-ce en faire un ou se tenir toujours en dehors ? Je crois que c'est se tenir en dehors dedans, en y étant, et y être ce n'est pas se tenir au-dessus du Mal mais dedans et être le Mal lui-même, le Mal qu'il y ait Dieu à rassasier, l'hymen de la Morgue qui est que le pli ne fut jamais un pli...

                        Antonin Artaud

TYMPAN: 1a: drum
                   b: a celtic bowed stringed musical instrument

                  2a: (obs.) TYMPANUM
                    b: any of various membranous plates functioning basically like the membranous tympanum of the ear.

                  3a: or TYMPAN SHEET: a sheet of material (as paper or cloth) in a printing press that is placed between the impression surface and the paper to be printed.

TYMPANUM: The tense double membrane separating the outer from the middle ear — tympanic membrane — called also eardrum.
                  A membrane in a sound-producing organ that acts as a resonator.

TYMPANIC NERVE: a branch of the glossopharyngeal nerve arising from the petrosal ganglion, distributed to the walls of the tympanum of the ear where it takes part in forming a plexus.

THE NEWT LIFE

> *Mas per melhs assire*
> *mon chan,*
> *vau cercan*
> *bos motz en fre*
> *que son tuir cargat e ple*
> *d'us estranhs sens naturals;*
> *mas no sabon tuich de cals.*
>
> Guiraut de Bornelh

Dee-doo, dee-dum.

No such thing
as a simple twist

Dee-da, dee-doo,
"What is it stammers
under the lintels of words

a breath of air"
Dee . Die .
        Die Dame Art
Amiss
    echoes of
hilaritas
(common salt
added to
the rarer gold
of cars rimas)
& never sad

thus spoke
the shuffled
words of cause.

    Re : birth
breath-sound
of the sun
coming
in the maiden.

   (the given
Doors
     tympan *&* hymen
oblique boundaries
of sound
       &,
         hammer-
headedness) the

"asunderwritten"
on the made bed
of fall or
fall's ore
     (gold) aurora
l'aura,
   autumn's *Atem* a
     breath
       breaking
on the unmade bed
    through
    taking
summer's hymn, her

maiden:
          had . done for .
                taking
it all in
to
   where
a newt life beckons.

Sap.
     Filling the gaps
my hollowed teeth & I
the cranky lion.
Lie low, sweet form.

Come again, come
fill her, ful-
fill the prostrate
prophecy.
          A
proffered apple that
won't bite
you who are
at this late twist re-
turned
from rust
to lust,
        (a verb
to dare win/ter
: thrice strapped
to the must
you miss
the music our

lion's share.
        Miss
the false air, *l'aura*
of pestilence,
etiological clouds
to be seeded
in a different
city.

Dee-doo, dee-dum,
no such thing
as a simple twist.

       In the middle
of the newt life
      winter
won over
time now time
enough to
choose & leave
a language
where
    "verb"
is a noun &
eye means
verge
   or urge
    a verge
cannot come
to mean.

       means to come by
— as if —
"to verb"
  was
    all
      there
was.

THE EAR

Strapped & sealed
he missed the music.
The spoils

for greed of which
the crew goes overboard
harvests nothing
but the languish of fishes.
Fool's gold
lure of *Muspelheim*,
shiny coin your
face rubbed out rubbed
down to the blank
stare of the sea's
surface.

While the stultified
ship shuttles on,
we follow its course
with eyes strained
no line links it
to a loom
it drifts
"with masts sung earthward"
set free in a space
where right side up
& upside down
no longer mean,
it weaves along

not ship not church
a shapeless shape.

Protected
by his hymened
tympanum
no longer
divided in his
attentions
— impregnable fortress —
the lion
listens,

    hears
the gyroscope
the only function
of his organ.

Strapped
to his stirrups
he swings
a hammer sounding
the walls.
    Follows
the echo's
threads &
careful not to
lean against
the shaky ramps
begins to explore
the beginnings of
his story.

Tympanum . Labyrinth . Hymen . Thread .

Advancing now
(standing
       walking
              dancing)
wrapped into
he moves
enveloped, never
to emerge again
the form of an ear
built around a dam
turning about
its internal wall.

Newt shape
of a city
he feels along
(a labyrinth
semi-circular canals
— semi-lunar)
           a city
wrapped
like a snail
around a floodgate
a dam
     stretching
towards the sea, closed
in upon itself
but open towards
the sea.

 Amazed
the lion finds
himself
on a beach
he bends down
to the other form
the female form
picks up
what the sea
spelled out a
shell
  full &
  emptied of its
  waters,
     anamnesis
of the sea's ear
the only sound
against
his ear.

 It happens,
has to happen
here . the crack
resounds,
   birth
of a language
a different song
"sexual jubilation
is a glottal choice of
a lunar canal
the clear auricular ringing
a clear instillation of
sound"

cracks
the wax seal
cuts the straps
   release
& the storm
abides.

PIERRE JORIS

ARTAUD / CELAN / JORIS

PRAYER

Blazeskulls give us, skulls
singed by heavensbeam,
clear-eyed, real and true,
rotted through by you.
Let us be the wombfruit of
the Innerheavens
abyss after abyss rip through us,
shove your nail into it,
let it be whirlwind and whiteheat.
We hunger
after quaking starspace:
still our hunger.
Pour our bloodtrack full
of starlavas.
Cut us loose.
Quarter us
with cutting blazehand.
Unlock for us
the firevault, where
one dies beyond death.
Make our brain reel
deep inside the known.
Rob us of our reason
with the fangs of the new
typhoon.

NOTE: This is a my reworking into English of Paul Celan's translation of Antonin Artaud's poem "Prière." It was first published in the Celan issue of the magazine ACT, accompanied by a little essay trying to explain Celan's reworking of this early Artaud poem. I'll let it stand here as is.

From: CANTO DIURNO #1

2:45 p.m.

second attempt at translating "Todtnauberg," Celan's encysted record of his 1967 meeting with Martin Heidegger (a disaster as far as Celan is concerned, according to most sources). Clearly Celan had hoped for something (the opening botany, arnica, eyebright, is of healing plants) which Heidegger did not (could not?) (would not?) provide: in the visitors' book he wrote a line "von einer Hoffnung, heute,/auf eines Denkenden / kommendes / Wort / im Herzen,". Then a walk on unevened, unplaned, ground where they walk singly ("Orchis und Orchis"), then in the car, later, driving back, more talk, rough talk ("Krudes") overheard by a third person, the driver. And then a harsher landscape, high-moor, log-paths or trails, humidity.

TODTNAUBERG

Arnica, eyebright, the
draft from the well with the
star-die on top,

in the
cabin

written in the book
— whose name did it record
before mine? —
in this book
the line about
a hope, today,

for a thinker's
word to come,
in the heart,

forest-sward, unevened,
orchis and orchis, singly,

crudeness, later, while driving,
clearly,

he who drives us, the man,
he listens in,

the half-
trod log-
trails in the highmoor,

humidity,
much.

[...]

[1986]

THE DREAM OF THE DESERT IN THE BOOK

I.

The book lies open
in all the hallways
in all the oases
in all the dreams
around every corner
behind every sanddune

in this dream too
you have to add a line
your place is between
the already written
& the unwritten,
in the white empty space.

In this dream
Stalin smiled, & Heidegger too
in this dream
cockroaches
scuttled from the book — but
it had to be written in, despite
the smiles.

A dream of a book
a dream of a desert in a book
a dream of a desert that runs from the book
a dream of a book and a desert
a dream of a desert in a book
a dream of sand through fingers

a dream of white
a dream of mica
a dream of fennecs
a dream of a desert spilling from the book
into and through the hallway and out the door.

And a voice said
write in the book
& you will be healed

a voice said a voice said

my middle my voice my will
write in the book

write the desert
the dream
write the sand the white write the running
dream the book.

II.

a dream of Stalin
a dream of Celan
a dream of parents
a dream of houses

in the first house Celan hides in a
   closet & Stalin bangs his big boots
   & stomps over the wooden floor

in the second house Celan escapes
   through the back-window & Stalin
   screams and tears at his mustaches

in the third house we are not. It
   is full to overflowing with all the
   parents, everybody's parents,
   Celan's & Stalin's & mine too.

In the fourth house there is a city in
   ruins. A moon stands above it.
   It is white, it is full. It has
   djebels & wadis on it. It is
   pouring with sand.

From: AN ALIFBAA

[ا]
Adam is said to have written a number of books three centuries before his death. After the Flood each people discovered the Book that was destined for it. The legend describes a dialogue between the Prophet Muhammad and one of his followers, who asked: 'By what sign is a prophet distinguished?'

'By a revealed book,' replied the Prophet.
'O Prophet, what book was revealed to Adam?'
'A, b…' And the Prophet recited the alphabet.
'How many letters?'
'Twenty-nine letters…'
'But, oh Prophet, you have counted only twenty-eight.'
Muhammad grew angry and his eyes became red.
'O Prophet does this number include the letter alif and the letter lam?'
'Lam-alif is a single letter…. he who shall not believe in the number of twenty-nine letters shall be cast into hell for all eternity.'

1.
and Alif has many seats
under which he is silent
though you cannot call it suffering
suffering rhymes with zero
at least initially
a sweet round perfection
as we like to draw it
doodling one into the other

(newspaper margins of the b&w middle fifties
at Mme Cavaiotti's where I wrote
or learned to daily at 5 p.m. whose husband
told me that in the last war (which wasn't
the last at all) he had been
forced to drink his piss from his boot
in the desert of Libya, his wife linking
zeroes, rounds, in the margins of the daily
"Wort," making, making writing

a chain of nothingness
that is something
and that is our fate und Fluch:

that we have to do something
          even to achieve the nothing
          even if only we doodle
ourselves through life
          while talking on the phone
          to someone doodling elsewhere
          while all we mumble are
          sweet nothings chains
          of linked zeroes
                  yet
step back &   focus shifts

    a shape emerges   from the space created

        by the two   circles'

intersections,

                    mandorla,
                              wherein stands
                 the shape of Celan's eye, of the fruit
of the almond tree,
                 there stood, maybe,
the names of the six kings
of Madyan, make up the letters
of the Arabic
alphabet.

          The nothing, where does it stand?
It stands outside the almond,
it stands in the shells
of the suffer'un
the zero-crescents
above & below

("Human curl, you'll not turn grey,
Empty almond, royal-blue")

fall away
as the almond looms,
yet remain as links
of a chain,
isthmus-claws
sew mandorla to
mandorla.

INTERGLACIAL NARROWS | HOMAGE TO CELAN

SHAKESPEARE'S SONNET #71, RE-ENGLISHED AFTER PAUL CELAN'S GERMAN VERSION WITHOUT CONSULTING THE ORIGINAL:

You should, once I'm gone, mourn only as long
as you hear the bell, the dark one, from the tower;
as long as it needs to tell the world:
He who lived with you went to live with the worms.

This I write, but you, having read it,
forget who wrote it. For look — I love you:
I wish I'd never been on your mind,
for when you think of me, sorrow steals upon you.

You should let — once your gaze rests upon these words,
once I'm dust, dust & no longer —
love become what I became,
and my name, do not speak it again:

The world, wise-eyed, already looks for your tears,
me, now gone, with you to taunt.

CF. CELAN'S SILBE SCHMERZ

an answer
        a handswer
   a hand / some
      swerve

TO P.C.

Paul,
if I may,
I brought you
here, to another
blacksoil earth,
cousin to, I
hope,
the black soil
of Czernowitz.

The meridians of,
because in,
us
humans never
travel in
straight
lines,
      they stutter,
wander off the
straight and narrow,
bending
sans breaking,
into tomorrow's
blood rich
marrow.

VIA CELAN, AGAIN

to ride over
        the you —
            the men —

the you-man hurdles

DEAR ROBERT, I

wake up in pre-
dawn Brooklyn,
make water, heat water, squeeze
lemon, crush home-grown (at Joseph's
on 68th between 3rd & Ridge) peppers
(cayenne), make first pot of coffee
(Peruvian organic medium roast) in
orange French press thermos, look out,
windy, rain while we slept, heavy
colored dreams we tell us
we had but don't remember
more of, take her hot lemon
& coffee to Nicole finishing
this past Sunday's *New York Times* in bed,
take my cups to my study
remembering last night's sweet
Mets win in Washington but really
listening as I have since I got up
to France Cul where Olivier Cadiot speaking
of his new Shakespeare translation playing right
now in a mise-en-scène by Thomas Ostermeier
at the Comédie française, says
"Il n'y a pas de vers français pour accueillir
le vers shakespearien aujourd'hui," which I
think is totally accurate as I put cups on
desk, pour first coffee, turn
to look out at white-
capped waves — nothing
melvillian, just normal fall
adjustment — can't yet see the anchored ships,

the leaves still all on the trees
in the Narrows Botanical Garden
across Shore Road,
wind tires or tortures them or tries to,
at least shakes them without spearing them so
a big white incongruous light shines through every
so often all the way from Staten Island
while all the way from
wherever I was in my sleep
to this moment of opening the red notebook
& unscrewing the black "Sailor" fountain pen
I have really thought of nothing else than
that this day
is your birthday, Robert —
many happy returns, joyeux anniversaire, Alles
Gute! before I'll turn (in a minute,
right after sending this off to you)
to the last three poems
from Celan's *Niemandsrose*
that remain to be translated so that on
this your birthday I may finish what I started
in Annandale 51 years ago under your guidance.
I raise my (by now second) cup (of Peruvian)
to you, dear friend.

                                                                Bay Ridge, 9/25/18

STRANGE FEELING as I proofread my notes for *Microliths They Are, Little Stones*: all these books I know of because Celan read them, lived with them, referred to them — but that I decide I can never read because it would take up too much of the time left me to live and read and write.

That I have to go elsewhere and can never settle in late 19th / early 20th century Bukowina, no matter how much I like & am familiar with beech trees. I'd miss the (wider, contemporary) forest for the trees.

But I will read Margaret Susman's *Das Buch Hiob*, which came out back in 1946, the same year I did.

EARLIER TODAY I SAW
an old atlas
floating down
the Verrazano Narrows.

Which had nothing
or something
to do with my surprise,
later today, seeing a
footnote
defined Celan as
"translator and poet Paul Celan"
(Rankine, Claudia
  Don't let me be lonely, p. 143)
& goes on:
"committed suicide in 1970"

floating down
the Seine,

for so many years,
my Atlas.

MY FIRST (I THINK, memory suggests, though I can't be sure) dream of Celan: in b&w we come out of a flat in Paris where we have been doing something the dream doesn't remember, Celan offers to take me somewhere, drop me off, can't go a certain way or do something because his legs are bad, I say no worry, let's go another way, he wants to stop to buy me a box of his favorite chocolates, we get into his car, an old V.W., but with steering wheel on the right, we stop at a traffic light and talk, the cars behind us toot their horns, the light has turned green (the only color spot in the dream) but Celan keeps talking. I wake up.

A POEM OR SOMETHING, A GIFT, A SONG, FOR PAUL CELAN AT 100.

Her hand giant shadow
— mit Bleistift
on ceiling with night
reading light
pillowed between us —
graphites an unseen
page, on which
I'll write, standing up
in the kitchen,
        the good, no
the best thing about
night is it is
always a pre-
dawn.
      It goes way back,
½ time between your birth
& now, I
with a double breath-
turn (yours & mine),
embarked —
        before take-off
           father had asked for
            a shakehand
(a poem is that
      you said and
then let go)   in
          not my mother-
              tongue
          in my future

                        language he knew but reversed
                from early 1945 camp
                        fires in another night,
a
darker one you
knew too.
            What had freed father,
            drew me over,
            (you already knew better
            had —August '49— heard
            Gordon Heath sing climbing
            jacob's ladder, "twice he sang it, at
            the beginning and at the end"
            & in between strange fruit
            & a fraught encounter with
            the blond Northerner still &
            always freed fascist "doing Paris"
            at your table in, not on, the échelle)

and we are climbing some kind of ladder
different for each as should be
                you to Paris
                        me to New York
                                both with faith only in no faith
the right to blaspheme
as first right left
                after the third reich fell then
                & now the first empire here
   is falling down
falling down.
                My first crossing
                        (between your visit to Heidegger

                                & your first trip to Berlin)
                    ferried me across the Charlie Gibbs
                          fracture zone a transform fault dis-
                              places the Mid-Atlantic Ridge,
lands me in a "thickness:
                to be understood from the geological,
                    and thus from the slow
                          catastrophes & the dreadful fault-
      lines of language ——"
            but it is there
in the faultlines that writing starts. You wrote:
  "Columbus,
     eyeing the autumn-
     colchis, the mother-
          flower,
                  murdered masts and sails. Everything
set forth,
    free," (but we ban
that late loser, found
& lost
    by people he murdered,
another, our, atonement, I, here still
fifty years after your death —
which is not that of the book, that buch-,
that buch-
stable staff as
the beech is as the tree is the book the Buche
from your Book
-ovina, the
        first book, the one that
has the autumn crocus
only only a secret echo

                of the literally timeless,
name of their *colchique*,
             our autumn crocus
                  called up by reality
to meet again in the imagination
of your city, my city
all gathered in
one stands brightly on no
hill but by the sea, even if a black
sea, even if Colchis
is & is not
         New York
from where I greet you
this morning
on your hundredth birth
day.

IV. Up to & Including the Virus

Diaretics 2020-2021

1/1/2020

The numbers add up
& bring it to us
minus or plus the world —

there's no more hiding
night has fallen
take my hand

time to get going
the numbers have been crunched &
they haven't run out as yet.

1/14

                        (in *Think Café*

with nothing to think about
except for wondering how
do you think, what is
the process? from outside
in or from inside out, or
is it what happens in
between (like everything
else) where outside
& inside meet or if
all goes (to the) well at
least confuse theirselves —

1/26

Misheard on radio (some ad seems to claim that
    "dying is a global culinary experience."

1/30

It is still night,
the words as yet as few
as there are lights
on the opposite shore

All shores are opposite
— but opposite what?

My eyes, no — they have to be in
my eyes for me to see,
they are opposite the night
and touch, the lights
are the night.

1/31

The great dying of the birds
puts cheap gas into your cars
& a feather on the hat
of this and that
"industry," celebrating
its adage, a dollar is
worth more than a life,
any life.

NOTE TO SELF ON 11 FEBRUARY

cell-sense   (N)
cell-self   (P)

the body politic of the
community of one's cells —
as place of reflection:

the cell & its relation to sugar —
N's contention that it, the cell,
will go for the easiest high, &
loves sugar — & by mimesis (? —
my word here) we, that organized bag
of cells do the same.
                I.E. life's like that, or that's life
goes for
the quick fix —

    & the birds love the fermented berries,
        getting loaded's a treat
            for them too!

FEBRUARY 14TH

no, I don't
love you

more today
than on any

of the other 364
days of the year.

2/15

day after, even even-
ing after,
      the coldest
morning of the winter,
sun out & clear skies,
cleansing February skies —
     the day after
love, love is still
 there, & here,
      it is always coming
       like the wave
        & the shore knows
        & stays put.

day after five cardinals
    on the Rambles,
     & one Cooper's hawk,
       day after morning
        after noon
          after evening,

     the three rafters of day
    to swing on,
live under —

2/16

The word of the day
the screen saver (or
Savior?) claims
is *soniferous*
        (according to Webster's meaning
        producing or conducting sound as in
        soniferous marine animals)
you say I am confused
is it today's word
that is soniferous
or is the word of the day
that word,
        I say I am confused as
I type the word it is auto-
magically (I tried to type -matically but it too was
retro-corrected) into
coniferous but then
        you break
through my confusion
saying "I am soniferous"
loudly,
        and the day
answers with light
laughter.

MONDAY FEB 24, 6:30 A.M.
                                         EST time on
                                         NY-AbuDhabi
flight
                              (5 hours sleep, wow:
long ago in
dream we
                crossed the Charlie Gibbs
                     fracture zone the transform fault
                                displaces the Mid-
Atlantic Ridge,
but now awake ahead as
on the map
we have just crossed
the Tigris
& the language
rightly so
veers to Arabic
again & again
no matter how often
or hard I hit
the English button,
but refreshes too
quickly for my rusty
decipherment of
that Alif baa to
give me the info
I want
the plane now halfway
over Basra
halfway over
the Gulf, history
old & new
rushes in.

2/29 : Leap year day,
spent leaping
continents on Etihad Airways
flight from Abu Dhabi to
NYCity after
strange yet happy days
at the Abu Dhabi St. Régis
celebrating friend Adonis'
90th with a flourish & grand
finale,
      & now, double leap,
doubled over in laughter
at the in-flight movie, a
French comedy called
Donne-moi des ailes, Give me
wings, which I wind
up folding in, to sleep
myself across the Charlie Gibbs
fracture zone that
            transform fault
folds me back in & gets me
home.

3/7
            Houston, Rice U
last day of Celan huis-clos, 11 of us in one room, no spectators,
no listeners, still, a pleasure to listen to those present. I rehearse
my ½ century with Celan's work, reading, thinking,
translating. Go back to the opening poem of *Breathturn*:

> YOU MAY confidently
> regale me with snow:
> as often as I strode through summer
> shoulder to shoulder with the mulberry tree,
> its youngest leaf
> shrieked.

& discuss my thinking about the German word "bewirten" explaining that "the second verse initially read 'treat me to snow' — but, on revising for publication, that seemed too American, too familiar, while 'regale me' is a bit more formal with its 2 syllables against 'treat's one though it still has one less than 'bewirten's 3." Then did the same with the German word "schrie," "which in English needs here to come as the last word of the poem, & which I first translated as 'cried.' That soon felt too lachrymose, not strong enough, even though 'shrieked' ends the poem on a higher pitch than the more placid German 'Blatt' — while however conserving the sound rhyme of schrie/shrieked, & so on. It is the pleasure & the agony of translation to always be caught in such a multiplicity of possibilities, none of which, you quickly learn, is final. Notice that this multiplicity can also affect the original: The written poem has 'schritt durch den Sommer' but in the reading you just heard, Celan says 'ging durch den Sommer.' 'Ging' is of course a much more familiar, common word than the slightly elevated or near-formal 'schritt.' And so, if the author himself sees fit to thus change register in the poem, maybe the translator can permit himself to revisit his previously discussed change & in a later edition go back to 'treat' rather than 'regale'?"

— Could possibly expand this into full essay on poetics with suggestion that writing & translating are basically the same activities, with not one fixed "original" in sight. Maybe when back. Meanwhile, what overshadows all, here now, is the coronavirus scare.

(remembering which, I spray my hands with Nicole's mixture).

3/11

Back home in what I've been calling a "self-imposed quarantine" in emails — wanting to stay in, unsure of the next move — or moves, I.E. what writing project to go to, & how to deal with this covid-moment.

....

A Shelter Is Not Necessarily An Island
as title for something cogent right now
comes to mind & brings to mind
Eric Mottram's 1971 book title
   Shelter Island & The Remaining World
    so now is shelter
the opposite of the
   "remaining world"
— when the remaining world is
helter-skelter (late 16th century adverb: a rhyming jingle of unknown
origin, perhaps symbolic of running feet or from
Middle English *skelte* 'hasten') —
  or not? No,
shelter is island
    island is always plural
is always already part of
    some
multiplicity, an archipelago
"a series of sound groups   a local thrush
   chickadees at their red plastic spinning bins
    active for dark brown striped white
sunflower seeds
gull's white crab and cree low over wrinkling shore planes"
     (E.M. *Shelter Island*)

3/18

The most difficult pivot of the day: away from the black composite computer desk, 180 degrees toward the old English wooden refectory table, this notebook & the view over the Narrows, my favorite. As if any minute could bring the news that the end of this scourge is in sight, or that the end is on the ticker of the screen. Meanwhile outside there are fewer cars and people, but there are cars and people moving in several opposite directions.

3/19

NY outbreak getting worse. Still a fair amount of people out there in our parks and jogging along the Narrows. Things look semi-normal, but I feel odd —

"I know my dreams are unreal
but they are my dreams"
                    E.M. "The Remaining World"

3/21

the silver water surface
love it
don't step on it

3/23

We took you, hawk,
for a red-tail, very
sorry, you were & are a cooper,
even though probably
immature.

3/24

Outside:
        sun caught
    in bare tree branches,
           cradled

Inside:
        me caught
    in shelter in place,
           cradled too

p.s. We shall both
    rise again

3/29

    Waiting for the reboot
    Turn to the window
    "Comfort" not yet in sight

3/30

Thinking of a possible essay on "commissure" that piece, that place conjoining Celan & Olson, I just came across this in an old notebook, 8 June 1971, London, a day on which I threw the I Ching & got:

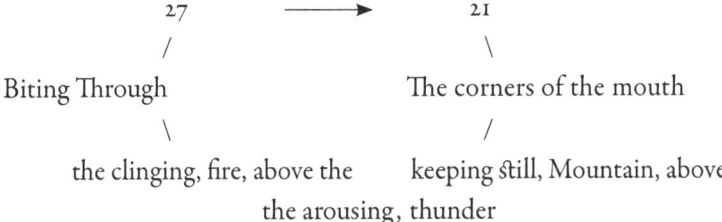

```
        27         ⟶         21
        /                     \
Biting Through        The corners of the mouth
        \                     /
  the clinging, fire, above the   keeping still, Mountain, above
              the arousing, thunder
```

3/31

We are only eternal while we are alive.

4/1

These buds on the branches
here this year too
their steadfastness . my surprise

*

Nachhaltige Nicht-Nachhaltigkeit
= title of a German book
translates as:
        sustainable non-sustainability
(or: the empire strikes back…)

*

From an early Carolyn Forché poem called "What it Cost":

    "As we will never know what it means,
    we will know what it costs."

4/3

awaiting slow green of first leaves
slowly stretching — your dawn saying on mind:
time is a bullfight

4/4

Two sparrows on a near branch
I bend over the page to get it down
— gone

4/5

All morning into early afternoon preoccupied with the dead person found under the pine-tree in the Narrows Botanical Garden right across the street under our windows.

                        Young guy in our building found the corpse — we had been wondering as we saw police huddled, delimiting the area with yellow tape, if it was a vagrant, possibly sick with Covid-19, an overdose, or what else. I did think for a brief moment that it could be a suicide. Later a black NYC van stopped, left again, returned. The coroner, no doubt. The body, covered by a white sheet or body-bag was all the more visible — for hours. The young man who found him confirmed (talking to Nicole window to sidewalk) that it was a suicide, most likely, middle-aged white male, not a vagrant, well-dressed, strange manner of death, i.e. hanging himself from a very low branch, body prone on ground. Possible murder? Execution? Can't find anything yet in the local news. Nicole lit a candle, as we wished him good travels through the barzakh.

*

During a zoom reading by Jerome Rothenberg

Two thousand run
of the mill Buddhas
tread water

There are no mirrors
anywhere in the world
: only others

In several parts
the whole
is & is not

The whole is
& is not
in separate parts

In acts of cruelty
the present is miscarried
again and again

Time you say is a bullfight
I say time is kneeling
in the sand hour before the bull

4/6

my first (I think; memory suggests, though I can't be sure) dream of Celan: in b&w we come out of a flat in Paris where we have been doing something the dream doesn't remember, Celan offers to take me somewhere, drop me off, can't go a certain way or do something because his legs are bad, I say no worry, let's go another way, he wants to stop to buy me a box of his favorite chocolates, we get into his car, an old V.W. but with steering wheel on the right, we stop at a traffic light and talk, the cars behind us toot their horns, the light has turned green (the only color spot in the dream) but Celan keeps talking. I wake up.

*

<blockquote>
birds courting in the tree
in which yesterday
a man hanged himself
</blockquote>

4/9

<blockquote>
For Nicou, Today of & for All Days…
</blockquote>

On *this* April day
there are (nearly)
never April showers —

the only one I remember
is an (imaginary?)
shower of rose-petals

eleven years ago on
the sunny April day
we I-do-'d each other

having already worked
hard at making it work
for nearly twenty Aprils

& happily those imaginary
rose-petals are becoming
more real day after day.

*

To write of my father as I think of him so much these days: washing my hands thoroughly several times a day not singing Happy Birthday but taking my rings off, he comes to mind, he who didn't wear rings, not even a wedding band, because of the daily often-repeated ritual of hand-washing & the pulling on of surgical gloves (which the rings, I have now experienced myself, can easily rip). And I tried to remember & then imitate his motions, hands held head-high palms facing backward, elbows out front push open door, one twists hot water faucet open, pushes down on soap-dispenser as other hand receives the soap (father used bars). As I watch my hands washing & washing there's a fade-out into the washbasin of the old Clinique Saint-Louis in Ettelbruck, corner of the avenues John F. Kennedy and Lucien Salentiny, my father's hands are doing these same movements while his voice explains to me how to do it & why it is necessary & tells me about Robert Koch, Alexander Fleming, Louis Pasteur & microbes & infections, & as he washes off the soap I see the little tear-shaped flesh excrescence at the tip of one (I cannot remember now which) small finger he tells me he got because he poked himself accidentally with an infected needle in a lab when studying medicine & he ends with the story of how he who as a young doctor knew about the newly arrived penicillin couldn't convince his father to take any when grandfather Joseph lay sick with what we would now call a basic strep-throat, & so Joseph's infection worsened & he died on 23 March 1942 in that same hospital at that time under German occupation called Sankt Ludwigs Klinik.

        I write this on my old wooden refectory table looking out at the Verrazano Narrows where every morning I can and most mornings do greet grandfather Joseph who just before or right after 1900 came up these Narrows in a Conradian ship sailing into New York Harbor a story he told my father who told it to me as he had passed 4 years before I was born. Ten days ago it was the USNS Comfort sailed up these same Narrows, reopening that path of memory, most likely laden with massive amounts of penicillin and its descendants — not that such anti-bacterials are of much use in the fight against the current virus.

4/12

So in the last dream,
Derrida comes down the
majestic red-carpeted
staircase just before day
breaks and with a
large smile & an even
more expansive wave
of his left arm
(the other rests on the
baluster) gives the
order for the gerrymandering
to begin or to end
I can't be sure how
this one links to the
long black and white
dream just before (only
a quick pee separates
them) in which I talked
lengthily to various politicians
and a few pundits
(me included, it seems)

about the evil of
gerrymandering, and
we are all absolutely
certain, as certain as one can
only be in a dream, that
our lives depend on
ending that terrifying
trend and now that I
woke up for good I
would really like to go
back into the last one
and ask Jacques if his
gesture meant to begin
or to end what the
dream proposed. But I
can't, I can't, the sun
has risen behind me
where I can't
see it though
I do see its reflection right
in front of me, reddening
the East Coast buildup
West of here and on
Staten Island just
across the Verrazano Straights
much more quiet today
these waters, not half as roiled
as yesterday or as my dreams
made me today.

4/14

So what is there left
except for the light
of a watery sun slanting
through clouds,

some cars, some runners
all wearing masks except
for those three in a circle
(what is a circle of three?)

((there is
no way of
squaring that one
except as the four-line
stanza, come in without asking
& now broken up))

based on 6 feet distance
who are smoking in concert
and that 5-kid family of
orthodox Jews rushing toward

the pier and maybe the water
will part and they can
escape the plagues of New York
— no pharaoh will chase them to no paradise.

4/22

        everything looks normal
        (from where I sit)
        but nothing is.

4/28

This morning's birds,
no owl in Owl's Head Park,
but
        6 or more
Northern Flickers (my first sighting
after Nicole's excited reports)
the usual mess of robins,
my gaggles of sparrows, some
common house, some white-
throated, some chirping balls
of white bellies stuck out &
red-brown Mohawk aimed at
the rising sun,
    the usual array of doves,
        never think of calling
them mourning, in or
out of same, they're just a
bit sad,
        but then a ring of doves
with capitals in English
but without in the Arabic
tawq al-hamanah is
a major treatise on love
by Ibn Hazm

(to be looked into
when home-in-shelter from
early morning birding
walk).

4/29

Merle Bachmann: "I am in exile from exile."

5/4

2-hour morning walk nets
a day to be named "Grey Catbird
Day" in honor of the multiple sightings
in Owls Head Park —
a walk ending w/ 7 cormorants off
Pier 69, & in between
one Eastern Towhee
any number of robins
one female cardinal
one "Elster" — ah, yes, magpie,
and all the sparrows,
all the sparrows!

5/11

Days ago
I wrote about a dove,
& thinking back on it
& Ibn Hazm's *Ring*

of same I turn
to the window
& there she is
on the branch of
the tree, keeping a cool
6 feet
social distance,
as I raise my head
& she's gone
except for the
cooing, still
hanging in the
air — even after the
sharp warning wing
whistle
      stopped.

5/18

Yahya Hassan: "I am the wandering target that returns fire."

5/19

"If you don't know
people younger than
you, you are dead."
Someone said something
like this, or quoted it
yesterday, or the day before,
I can't remember, because
I'm getting older,

but not dead yet,
as the person I heard say
this was certainly younger
than me,
& I listened to him.

5/20

"What knows you, infects you."
                    Edwin Torres

"Aware horses change
 riders midstream"
                    George Quasha

"You're not my fate
 you're my choice"
                    Nicole Peyrafitte

5/22

"La poésie, c'est l'amande,
 le reste, du commentaire."

"Poetry is the almond,
 everything else, commentary."

            Albert Memmi (who died this very day at age 99)

*

We always say
he or she died —,
that can be 700 years
ago in the
past or today in what we call
the present, tho not that tense,
tho some times we say s/he is dying,
tho that refers always to something will
happen in the future.
                      We never say s/he dies today,
a present tense would sound like
a future, no, dying's always
in the past,
           always has happened already
is never more than someone else
's memory of a past event — as
if you will never die
but have always already
done so in the past.

                    (added in the future / present, pre-
                      paring this book for publication, 7/2/22)

5/31

To think through a new biology, another
angle situates hss (homo sap sap):
      world ⟶ hu/man ⟵ world

I.E. surrounded by world in & out-
      side:

cells in/of human body total: 30 trillion
bacteria inside human body
I.E. human microbiome: 38 trillion

6/2

Woke up with lines from an old poem
& the image of the kingfisher we
saw yesterday morning in mind:
  Olson's *Kingfisher* & Mao's quote: La
lumière / de l'aurore / est devant
vous!
  & later: nous devons /
nous lever / et agir.
      From a speech
given December 1947, sets
le la de ce jour,
  the tone of my day, today.

Those two 3-steps
now came back with me thinking
not of sunrise, dawn, new be-

ginnings & this for me, for my
new language, being in the
West of my birthlands, in America
— the alpha male, the rich, the bitter —
but now at 73, of sunset, dusk,
a coming darkness, but not
mine as much as of
that of the new country I had
chosen back then, this America,
the morning after this
bad excuse for a president as much as
declares it, the country, under
military control.

Has the will to change
changed?
    Or is it only
my own old age pulling me
down? No dawn
left?
   I did see the
kingfisher as black
& white,
    perched
on the rusted remains
of a ½ sunk steel
structure in Calvert Vaux
Park. It took off
who knows whereto — but
showed no ill will on no ill wind
   of change.

6/3

History is written after the catastrophes.
                                Bertolt Brecht

6/4

Darling's Curve

I'm confused,
it's not portly
Ronnie
   I see, I mean
hear,

brilliantly
commenting on an early spring
game,
      but a skinny,
sharp-looking (even in those
outdated uni-
forms)
      dude throwing
(me
      a curve all
the way from that
80's game into
my tired mitt, this
mid-morning
    — too early or too late? —
in my shelter-at-
         home-base
living room,
& I'm happy
  to be an armchair catcher
    this covid morn
rather than a flailing
      bat out in the
        world.

6/27

    work ⎫
The poet's walk ⎬ not a line, not
even a or his ⎭
      meridian. No: a border / frontier
that is, a territory; a width —

— overheard on radio (France Culture:
>	image of poem
as handful of Mikado sticks
dropped on table, needing
to be moved to be read.

*

"allergie aux chefs de rayons de la poésie"
allergic to the department supervisors of poetry, she who said it, is:
>	Liliane Giraudon

*

mother tongue /
>	other tongue
langue-mère /
>	Langue ère

*

the idea of purity of language is as ideologically fraught as that of purity of race, country, nationality.   The only thing that makes life possible is the meeting of different elements — they create life (not some white-bearded old guy)   The only thing that makes the poem possible is that same meeting of different elements — a meeting that creates a tension — a tension that makes sparks fly — sparks that light up our nights a little bit — or more if we learn how to keep the sparks flying.

7/9

Thinking on Batty Weber essay:
        maybe around the fact that
   language is political
        How then to justify my choice
   of the late 20C most imperialistic language?

7/11

"memory is like a dog that lays down
wherever it wants."
                Cees Nooteboom
                (opening page of *Rituale*)

"…where it pleases." (official translation in
                Good Reads)

7/16

        Predawn Poetics Haiku with German *Einlagen*

The poem, rarely, a *Hauptsatz*.
More often & better, a *Nebensatz*.
At best, however, a *Danebensatz*.

*

At 8:43 a.m.
  On looking out
    through my father's eyes
or rather through
  his Hensoldt

Wetzlar   Nacht   Dialit (?
            8 × 56B
slightly longer, much
  heavier than today's
     binoculars —
I remember his gesture,
  carefully pulling them up with
     right hand to eye level
while left hand & arm
  flung back shush little
     me out
hunting with him, mid-fifties
  early fall forests, looking
     for deer at wood's rim
just found & verified by
  those binoculars I now pull
     up to my eyes
at Plumb Beach early summer
  morning to verify the
     bird is indeed an oyster
catcher. Dad would love
  to be here this morning.
     He is.

8/13

                Paradise is

           where land meets sea

           where the outside
              of our bodies

                meets the
                 inside

9/14

On September 14th, Dante's Death Day

gone for 700 years
    leaving us here, in the
        middle kingdom

   Purgatory
which was Paradise once
        but which we soiled

   and are about to
turn into hell, or
       at least an Inferno

for homo sapiens, the
    disappearing species
        — if it comes to that —

there's life
    left, there will be
life left

    and right
it will move
       on, even without us

it will rejoice in us
  gone — I can hear the
    birds celebrating

                    the trees too
                            the air cooling
                                    the sea cooling

                    it will be the real paradise
            the one sans-sapiens,
that arrogant inter-

ference!

11/18

You cannot look forward
to your birth year
you can only look back
on it, as it becomes
visible. as you leave
it, as
the years pass & you
grow older.

Do not forget it.
I mean the birth year,
that anchors you in
this world that is
cave & light,
learn to read the
drawings on its
walls, they are
your entry.

*

watching
        those many
sparrows
        bouncing
                around
the hedge &
        fence takes
a lot of
        eyegility.

12/6

that was the last leaf
on that branch

falling

& not a bird
taking flight

12/20

at 10:59 this morning
the sun stood still
had reached the Tropic
of Capricorn just as
I held out my arm
for my second Moderna
booster shot.

The side-effects on arm
& self seem minimal at
best, the sun, the sun
will make our days longer

as it moves again, & I
start a new notebook
with many questions happily
or unhappily, ¿quien sabe?,
unresolved, with a tough
six months ahead. Keep
believing in the sun as it
moves & grows & makes
more light day by day.

12/23

the weather holds.
Will I?

12/24

Final interview question from Florent for our book, to be retitled *Always the Many, Never the One: Conversations In-between* — a question he essentially articulated around my concept/practice of the in-between.   Need to add that to be in the in-between means that you cannot take the p.o.v. of the overview, overlook, top of the mountain — that single God's eye view that would see it all. Haraway's "God's p.o.v. = God's trick." We have two eyes, at least — to which we give too much credit, as is. Remember that every pore of your skin is an eye, is proprioceptive, an in-between that is / has to be both exteroceptive & interoceptive.

OTHER BOOKS BY PIERRE JORIS

The Irritation Ditch (Parentheses Writing Series, 1991)
Janus (St. Lazaire Press, 1988)
Breccia: Selected Poems 1972–1986 (PHI, 1987)
Good-bye to England (Loot, 1987)
Net/Work (Spanner Editions, 1983)
The Book of Luap Nalec (Ta'wil Books, 1982)
make it up like say (1982)
Tracing (Arc Press, 1982)
The Broken Glass (Pig Press, 1980)
Old Dog High Q (Writers Forum, 1980)
Body Count (Twisted Wrist, 1979)
The Tassili Connection (Ta'wil Press, 1978)
Tanith Flies (Ta'wil Books, 1978)
Hearth-Work (Hatch Books, 1977)
Antlers I–XI (New London Pride, 1975)
A Single-minded Bestiary (poet & peasant, 1974)
Trance/Mutations (1972)
The Fifth Season (Strange Faeces Press, 1971)

PROSE

Arabia (Not So) Deserta (Essays on Maghrebi & Mashreqi Writing & Culture) (Spuyten Duyvil, 2019)
Adonis & Pierre Joris, *Conversations in the Pyrenees* (Contra Mundum, 2019). Bilingual edition
The Agony of I.B. (Éditions PHI, 2016). Theater
Justifying the Margins (Salt, 2009)
A Nomad Poetics (Wesleyan U.P., 2003)
Global Interference (Liberation Press, 1981)
The Book of Demons (with Victoria Hyatt, as Joseph W. Charles) (Simon & Schuster, 1975)
The Entropy Caper (1973). Radio play
Another Journey (1972)

ANTHOLOGIES

The University of California Book of North African Literature (Vol. 4 in the *Poems for the Millennium* series), co-edited with Habib Tengour (UCP, 2012)
Poems for the Millennium, Vols I–II (with Jerome Rothenberg) (U.C.P., 1995 & 1998)
Joy! Praise! A Festschrift for Jerome Rothenberg (Ta'wil Books, 1991)
Poésie Internationale : Anthologie (with Jean Portante) (Editions Guy Binsfeld, 1987)
Matières d'Angleterre (with Paul Buck) (In'hui, 1984)

EDITED BOOKS

A City Full of Voices: Essays on Robert Kelly, ed. by Pierre Joris with Peter Cockelbergh & Joel Newberger (CMP, 2020)
A Voice Full of Cities: The Collected Essays of Robert Kelly, ed. by Pierre Joris & Peter Cockelbergh (CMP, 2013)
Claude Pélieu, *La Crevaille* (Posthumous Writings of Claude Pélieu, transcribed & edited by Pierre Joris (Paris: collection *Ressacs*, Editions de l'Arganier, 2008)
Paul Celan: Selections, Poets for the Millennium Series (University of California Press 2005)
The Burial of the Count of Orgaz and Other Writings of Pablo Picasso (with Jerome Rothenberg) (Boston: Exact Change, 2004)
pppppp: The Selected Writings of Kurt Schwitters (with Jerome Rothenberg) (Temple University Press, 1993). Re-issued by Exact Change in 2002.
Joy! Praise! *A Festschrift for Jerome Rothenberg on the Occasion of his Sixtieth Birthday* (Encinitas: Ta'wil Books & Documents, 1991)

TRANSLATIONS

    Mohammed Khaïr-Eddine, *Agadir* (with Jake Syersak) (Dialogos, 2020)

    Paul Celan, *Microliths They Are, Little Stones: Posthumous Prose* (Contra Mundum Press, 2020)

    Paul Celan, *Memory Rose into Threshold Speech: The Collected Earlier Poetry* (FSG, 2020)

    Safaa Fathy, *Revolution Goes Through Walls*, (SplitLevelTexts, 2018)

    Breathturn Into Timestead: The Collected Later Poetry of Paul Celan (FSG, 2013)

    Exile is My Trade: A Habib Tengour Reader, ed. & tr. by P.J. (BWP, 2012)

    Paul Celan, *The Meridian. Final Version — Drafts — Materials* (Stanford UP, 2011)

    Jukebox hydrogène de Allen Ginsberg (avec Nicole Peyrafitte) (2008)

    Paul Celan, *Selections* (UCP, 2005)

    Paul Celan, *Lightduress* (Green Integer, 2005)

    The Burial of the Count of Orgaz and Other Writings of Pablo Picasso (Exact Change, 2004)

    Abdelwahab Meddeb, *The Malady of Islam* (Basic Books, 2003)

    4 x 1: Works by Rilke, Tzara, Duprey & Tengour, tr. by Pierre Joris (Inconundrum Press, 2002)

    Paul Celan, *Threadsuns* (Sun & Moon Press, 2000)

    Michel Bulteau, *Crystals to Aden* (Duration Press, 2000)

    Habib Tengour, *Empedocles's Sandal* (Duration Press, 1999)

    Paul Celan, *Breathturn* (Sun & Moon Press, 1995)

    pppppp: The Selected Writings of Kurt Schwitters (with Jerome Rothenberg (Temple U.P., 1993)

    From the Desert to the Book: Interviews with Edmond Jabès (Station Hill Press, 1989)

Maurice Blanchot, *The Unavowable Community* (Station Hill Press, 1988)

Lune faucon de Sam Shepard (Christian Bourgois, 1987)

Horse's Neck de Pete Townshend (Christian Bourgois, 1986)

Motel Chronicles de Sam Shepard (Christian Bourgois, 1985)

Sentiments élégiaques américains de Gregory Corso (Christian Bourgois, 1977)

Mexico City Blues de Jack Kerouac (Christian Bourgois, 1977; reprint, Collection "poésie," Gallimard, 2022)

Temporal Flight by Jean-Pierre Duprey (earthgrip press, 1976)

Chants de la Révolution de Julian Beck (Christian Bourgois, 1975)

Contretemps à temps de Carl Solomon (Christian Bourgois, 1974)

COLOPHON

INTERGLACIAL NARROWS

was handset in InDesign cc.

The text font is *Garamond Premier*.
The display font is *Migra*.

Book design & typesetting: Alessandro Segalini

Cover design: CMP
Cover art: Nicole Peyrafitte

INTERGLACIAL NARROWS

is published by Contra Mundum Press.

Contra Mundum Press · New York · London · Melbourne

CONTRA MUNDUM PRESS

Dedicated to the value & the indispensable importance of the individual voice, to works that test the boundaries of thought & experience.

The primary aim of Contra Mundum is to publish translations of writers who in their use of form and style are *à rebours*, or who deviate significantly from more programmatic & spurious forms of experimentation. Such writing attests to the volatile nature of modernism. Our preference is for works that have not yet been translated into English, are out of print, or are poorly translated, for writers whose thinking & æsthetics are in opposition to timely or mainstream currents of thought, value systems, or moralities. We also reprint obscure and out-of-print works we consider significant but which have been forgotten, neglected, or overshadowed.

There are many works of fundamental significance to *Weltliteratur* (& *Weltkultur*) that still remain in relative oblivion, works that alter and disrupt standard circuits of thought — these warrant being encountered by the world at large. It is our aim to render them more visible.

For the complete list of forthcoming publications, please visit our website. To be added to our mailing list, send your name and email address to: info@contramundum.net

Contra Mundum Press
P.O. Box 1326
New York, NY 10276
USA

OTHER CONTRA MUNDUM PRESS TITLES

2012 *Gilgamesh*
      Ghérasim Luca, *Self-Shadowing Prey*
      Rainer J. Hanshe, *The Abdication*
      Walter Jackson Bate, *Negative Capability*
      Miklós Szentkuthy, *Marginalia on Casanova*
      Fernando Pessoa, *Philosophical Essays*
2013 Elio Petri, *Writings on Cinema & Life*
      Friedrich Nietzsche, *The Greek Music Drama*
      Richard Foreman, *Plays with Films*
      Louis-Auguste Blanqui, *Eternity by the Stars*
      Miklós Szentkuthy, *Towards the One & Only Metaphor*
      Josef Winkler, *When the Time Comes*
2014 William Wordsworth, *Fragments*
      Josef Winkler, *Natura Morta*
      Fernando Pessoa, *The Transformation Book*
      Emilio Villa, *The Selected Poetry of Emilio Villa*
      Robert Kelly, *A Voice Full of Cities*
      Pier Paolo Pasolini, *The Divine Mimesis*
      Miklós Szentkuthy, *Prae, Vol. 1*
2015 Federico Fellini, *Making a Film*
      Robert Musil, *Thought Flights*
      Sándor Tar, *Our Street*
      Lorand Gaspar, *Earth Absolute*
      Josef Winkler, *The Graveyard of Bitter Oranges*
      Ferit Edgü, *Noone*
      Jean-Jacques Rousseau, *Narcissus*
      Ahmad Shamlu, *Born Upon the Dark Spear*
2016 Jean-Luc Godard, *Phrases*
      Otto Dix, *Letters, Vol. 1*
      Maura Del Serra, *Ladder of Oaths*
      Pierre Senges, *The Major Refutation*
      Charles Baudelaire, *My Heart Laid Bare & Other Texts*

2017	Joseph Kessel, *Army of Shadows*
	Rainer J. Hanshe & Federico Gori, *Shattering the Muses*
	Gérard Depardieu, *Innocent*
	Claude Mouchard, *Entangled — Papers! — Notes*
2018	Miklós Szentkuthy, *Black Renaissance*
	Adonis & Pierre Joris, *Conversations in the Pyrenees*
2019	Charles Baudelaire, *Belgium Stripped Bare*
	Robert Musil, *Unions*
	Iceberg Slim, *Night Train to Sugar Hill*
	Marquis de Sade, *Aline & Valcour*
2020	*A City Full of Voices: Essays on the Work of Robert Kelly*
	Rédoine Faïd, *Outlaw*
	Carmelo Bene, *I Appeared to the Madonna*
	Paul Celan, *Microliths They Are, Little Stones*
	Zsuzsa Selyem, *It's Raining in Moscow*
	Bérengère Viennot, *TrumpSpeak*
	Robert Musil, *Theater Symptoms*
	Miklós Szentkuthy, *Chapter on Love*
	Charles Baudelaire, *Paris Spleen*
2021	Marguerite Duras, *The Darkroom*
	Andrew Dickos, *Honor Among Thieves*
	Pierre Senges, *Ahab (Sequels)*
	Carmelo Bene, *Our Lady of the Turks*
	Fernando Pessoa, *Writings on Art & Poetical Theory*
2022	Miklós Szentkuthy, *Prae, Vol. 2*
	Blixa Bargeld, *Europe Crosswise: A Litany*
	Pierre Joris, *Always the Many, Never the One*

SOME FORTHCOMING TITLES

Kari Hukkila, *1000 & 1*
Gabriele Tinti, *Bleedings*

AGRODOLCE SERIES ÆD

2020   Dejan Lukić, *The Oyster*
2022   Ugo Tognazzi, *The Injester*

HYPERION
On the Future of Æsthetics
2006–2022

To read samples and order current & back issues of *Hyperion*, visit contramundumpress.com/hyperion

Edited by Rainer J. Hanshe & Erika Mihálycsa (2014 ~)

CONTRA MUNDUM PRESS

is published by Rainer J. Hanshe
Typography & Design: Alessandro Segalini

THE FUTURE OF KULCHUR
A PATRONAGE PROJECT

LEND CONTRA MUNDUM PRESS (CMP) YOUR SUPPORT

With bookstores and presses around the world struggling to survive, and many actually closing, we are forming this patronage project as a means for establishing a continuous & stable foundation to safeguard our longevity. Through this patronage project we would be able to remain free of having to rely upon government support &/or other official funding bodies, not to speak of their timelines & impositions. It would also free CMP from suffering the vagaries of the publishing industry, as well as the risk of submitting to commercial pressures in order to persist, thereby potentially compromising the integrity of our catalog.

CAN YOU SACRIFICE $10 A WEEK FOR KULCHUR?

For the equivalent of merely 2–3 coffees a week, you can help sustain CMP and contribute to the future of kulchur. To participate in our patronage program we are asking individuals to donate $500 per year, which amounts to $42/month, or $10/week. Larger donations are of course welcome and beneficial. All donations are tax-deductible through our fiscal sponsor Fractured Atlas. If preferred, donations can be made in two installments. We are seeking a minimum of 300 patrons per year and would like for them to commit to giving the above amount for a period of three years.

WHAT WE OFFER

Part tax-deductible donation, part exchange, for your contribution you will receive every CMP book published during the patronage period as well as 20 books from our back catalog. When possible, signed or limited editions of books will be offered as well.

WHAT WILL CMP DO WITH YOUR CONTRIBUTIONS?

Your contribution will help with basic general operating expenses, yearly production expenses (book printing, warehouse & catalog fees, etc.), advertising and outreach, and editorial, proofreading, translation, typography, design and copyright fees. Funds may also be used for participating in book fairs and staging events. Additionally, we hope to rebuild the *Hyperion* section of the website in order to modernize it.

From Pericles to Mæcenas & the Renaissance patrons, it is the magnanimity of such individuals that have helped the arts to flourish. Be a part of helping your kulchur flourish; be a part of history.

HOW

To lend your support & become a patron, please visit the subscription page of our website: contramundum.net/subscription

For any questions, write us at: info@contramundum.net

www.ingramcontent.com/pod-product-compliance
Lightning Source LLC
Chambersburg PA
CBHW031319160426
43196CB00007B/588